To Elle,

grounded in His *love*

life made beautiful

God's love never fails!

♡

CONNIE SMITH

Connie Smith

Grounded in His Love: Life Made Beautiful

Text and photographs copyright © 2016 by Connie Smith

First Edition: November 2016

ISBN: 978-0-9906651-4-4

Library of Congress Control Number: 2016911176

1. Inspiration 2. Purpose 3. Hope 4. Encouragement 5. Love 6. Spirituality
I. Smith, Connie II. Grounded in His Love

Grounded in His Love may be purchased at special quantity discounts for sales promotions, premiums, corporate programs, gifts, and fundraising. For pricing information or to have Connie speak at your event, call 615-496-7006 or send an email to connie@neverloseheart.com.

Scriptures taken from the Holy Bible, New International Version®, NIV®. Copyright © 1973, 1978, 1984, 2011 by Biblica, Inc.™ Used by permission of Zondervan. All rights reserved worldwide. www.zondervan.com The "NIV" and "New International Version" are trademarks registered in the United States Patent and Trademark Office by Biblica, Inc.™

Editor: Dave Carew
Designer: Cheryl Casey
Author Photograph: Todd Adams
Publisher: Never Lose Heart LLC

Printed in China.

www.neverloseheart.com

He is before all things,

and in Him all things hold together.

Colossians 1:17

Dedication

This book is dedicated to the glory of the everlasting Rock who is my firm foundation, my refuge, and my strength. I am forever grateful for Your unfailing love and amazing grace.

Special thanks to the many people who have walked with me on this journey. I am beyond blessed to have family and friends with such loving and generous spirits who have enriched my life, prayed for me, given me words of wisdom, and offered their suggestions, enthusiasm, and feedback on this project. You know who you are, and I thank God for each one of you.

preface

The most beautiful part of life is not what we see on the outside, but knowing who we are on the inside. At the core of our existence, we all share a need to feel significant and valued. In our search for this fulfillment, we often take roads that look promising, but only lead to dead ends or danger zones, leaving us disappointed and longing for more. In a world filled with instability and broken promises, it can be easy to let hopelessness, fear, and despair set in. But there's a love that stands at the door of our hearts and knocks. A love with no strings attached. A love that gives purpose, meaning, and direction. A love that leads us to become the best version of ourselves.

This love became evident to me at a time in my life when I desperately needed to see the hope on the other side. I knew there had to be more to life than what I had been experiencing and had previously known. As I began to face my struggles and disappointments head-on, and as I began to seek greater meaning and purpose with anticipation, life began to open up to me in a whole new way. One by one, messages of hope, encouragement, and comfort began flooding my path in the form of random hearts. The more hearts I encountered, the more significant they became in my life—a confirmation of God's presence and His unconditional, relentless love. This deluge of love was so powerful and brought such life to the desolate places of my soul, that I knew it was not just for me. It was to be shared with the world. And that is how my first book, *Never Lose Heart,* came to be—born out of my journey and inspired by snapshots of my encounters with God's love.

The journey that led to *Never Lose Heart* encompassed such a variety of heart images in all types of places and entities—sidewalks, streets, food, tree bark, tree stumps, shrubs, plants, rocks, industrial materials, my cat's litter box, and even my own hand (after an accidental burn in the kitchen!). I love God's sense of humor and how He can speak in the most unexpected ways.

Interestingly, the hearts I began finding after the publication of *Never Lose Heart* were very similar to each other and without variety. Most of them were on the pavement of streets and sidewalks—all neutral in color. Each day I went for a walk, I would make a conscious effort to look up, thinking

I might discover a heart in the clouds. But my eyes would always shift back to the ground, as another heart caught my attention in my peripheral vision. I kept snapping photos for my collection, hoping to write another book, but honestly, the photo content wasn't terribly interesting (at that time). While I consider each heart to be a love letter from God and a gift to be cherished, it still seemed odd that I kept finding heart after heart on the ground. What happened to God's creativity? So one day I said to Him, "God, thank You for continuing to show me signs of Your love—no doubt these hearts are from You. I'm not sure if You want me to write another book, but if You do, don't You think we need some variety?" The very second I asked this question, it hit me like a ton of bricks that maybe there was a reason He was showing me so many hearts on the ground, and instantly the title came to me—*Grounded in His Love*. Shortly thereafter, the hearts on the ground came to life in various colors, textures, and backgrounds—a confirmation that indeed there was another message to be shared. And, little did I know, this message would build on the first one.

There is a perfect love that knows us better than we know ourselves and wants to lead us to places we never dreamed of. We can choose to see this love around us, but what value is it if we don't allow it to take root in our hearts? The fullness of life is not about how hard we strive or about finding an easy and comfortable place to land. It's about becoming. It's about discovering. It's about coming to know the love that first loved us. It's about allowing this love to rule in our hearts and shape our lives, one chapter at a time.

Wherever you may be on your journey, I hope this book will give you deeper insights into God's heart for you and the power of letting His love reign in your life. You were made for greatness, and this world needs you—the best version of you, grounded in His love.

introduction

To be still with God is to know God.
To know God is to know His love.
To know His love is to trust His love.
To trust His love is to be grounded in His love.
To be grounded in His love is to discover the fullness of who we were created to be.

Grounded in His Love is based on a scriptural viewpoint of God's heart and meant to be read like a personal love letter from God. My hope is that you will read it slowly, taking time to reflect and meditate on each message, and that these messages will take root deep within your soul, leading you to greater beauty and purpose in your life.

With a few exceptions, all the images in this book were taken with my iPhone, unaltered and just as I found them.

You may be aware of My existence, but do you know My heart for you?

I have loved you with
the purest love since the
beginning of time.

I have known the depth of your heart even before you were conceived.

Your life was not by chance
or without intent.

You were set apart for plans
that were made only for you.

All your days have been imprinted
with significant purpose...

and wrapped with My presence.

I have gone a great distance
to demonstrate My love for you…

by laying down My life for you…

to mark you blameless and free.

You are My treasure.

I will never stop pursuing you,
even in the shadows…

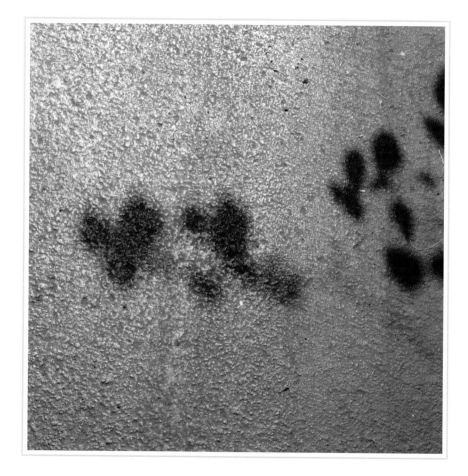

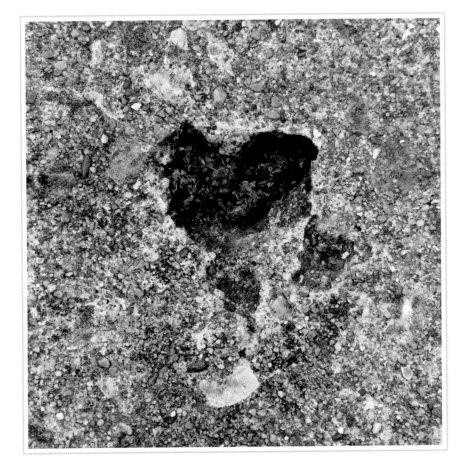

because I long to be with you
and fill your heart.

Like a river that never runs dry,
My love will never run out.

It breaks through walls
of fear and restores what's
been lost or broken.

It awakens dreams and
uncovers passions deep within.

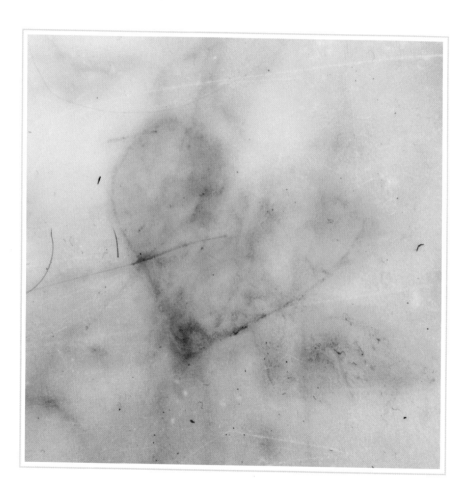

It gives power over the snares
that can so easily entangle...

and brings joy and vitality
to dying places.

My love makes all things new.

You don't have to climb a
mountain to find it…

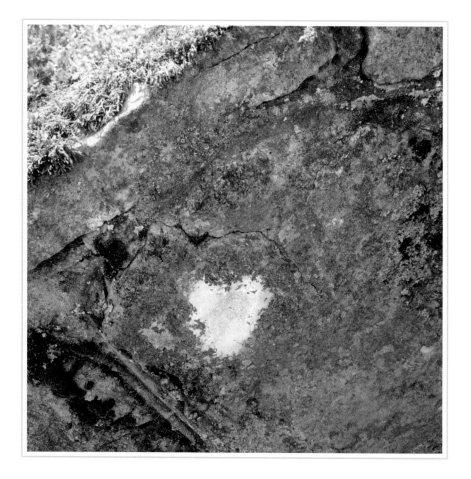

or polish your rough edges
to receive it.

Just believe.

I know every road you have traveled and every roadblock you have encountered.

I have seen every tear and heard every cry.

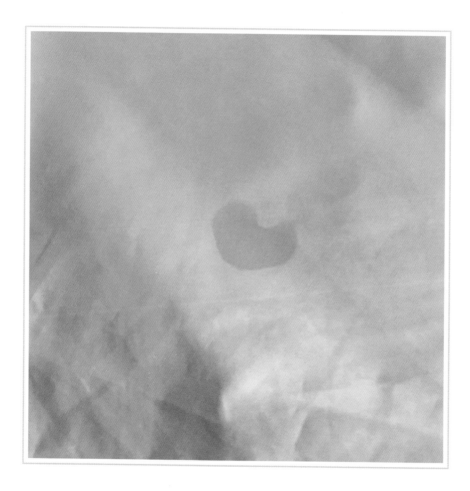

I understand the depth of your struggles and pain because I have walked these paths too.

Your disadvantages, disappointments, and failures do not define you or outline your future…

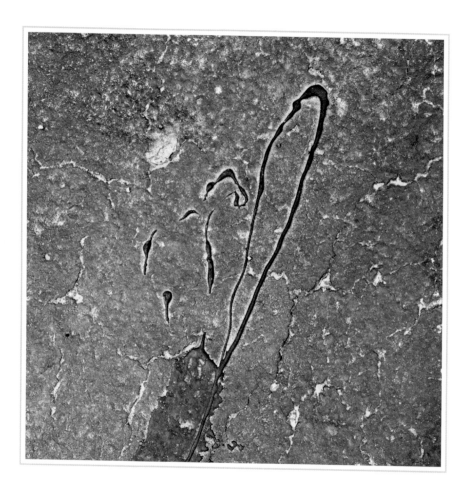

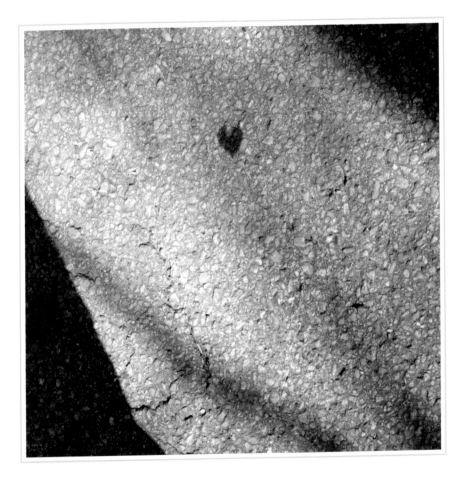

and your afflictions are not
the end of the road.

Your trials are only there to
propel you to the other side...

and bring you closer to
the beautiful person I've
created you to be.

My radiant beauty lives
in you because you were
created in My image.

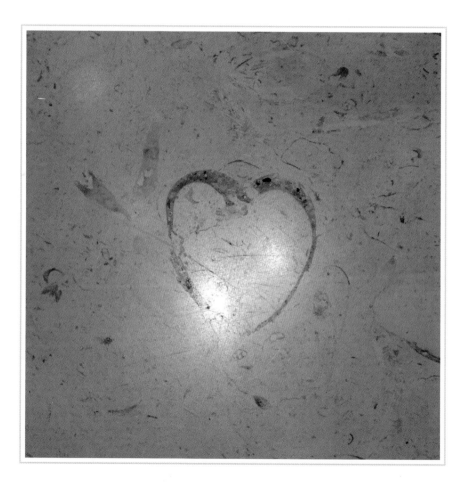

You are worthy.

So throw rejection, shame,
and the world's expectations
to the curb...

and stop dwelling on the
mistakes, flaws, and regrets
weathering your soul.

My heart does not keep
a record of your wrongs…

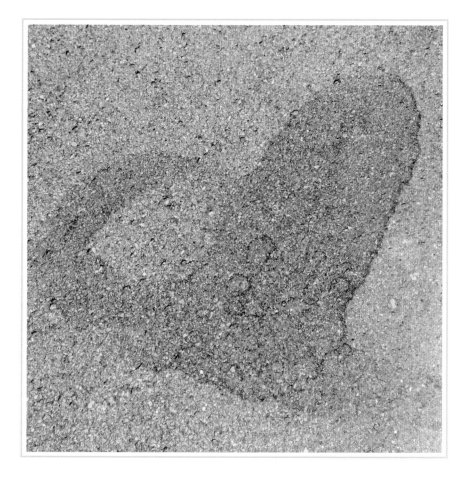

because My love is not based on your performance or how well you measure up.

My voice is the one that
builds up...

and cancels the lies that
want to tear down.

Choose to see My unconditional
love for you...

and let it take root deep
within you.

I can turn your stumbling blocks
into stepping stones…

and break the patterns that
have imprisoned you.

As you shed all you are
holding on to, My love will make
you more complete.

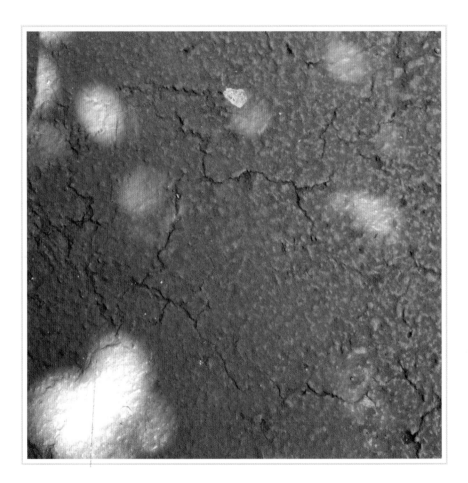

The more you seek Me,
the more your true self will shine.

Old desires will pale in
comparison to the new desires
I will put into your heart.

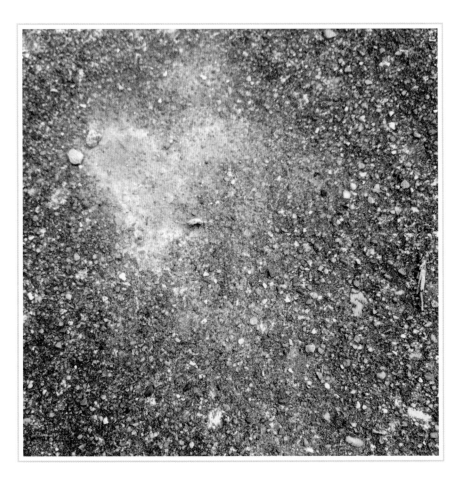

My plans for you are filled
with beauty, vibrancy,
abundance, and adventure
beyond your imagination...

because I am not bound by the limits of possibility that you see.

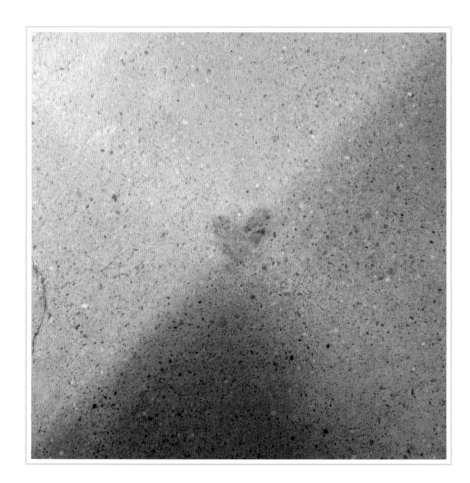

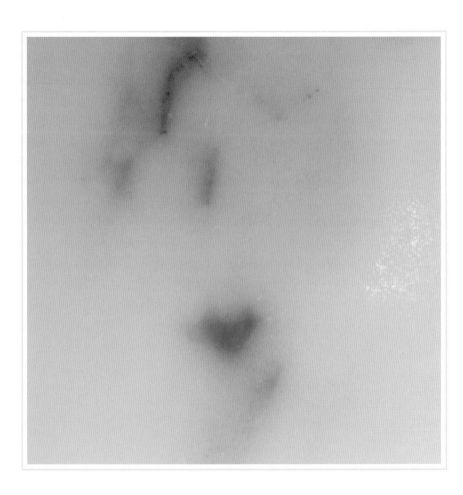

The path won't always be
black and white or crystal clear…

and there will be curves you
don't see coming…

but have faith.

I see the journey ahead and
will reveal all you need to know
in My perfect timing.

If I am faithful in providing for the birds of the air, how much more will I care for you?

All the "whys" will one
day make sense.

So…center yourself in Me,
and I will center Myself in you.

I am your Rock—the same yesterday, today, and forever.

My strength is made
perfect in your deficiencies
and imperfections.

My light will always lead you
and give you security, even as
the darkness grows around you.

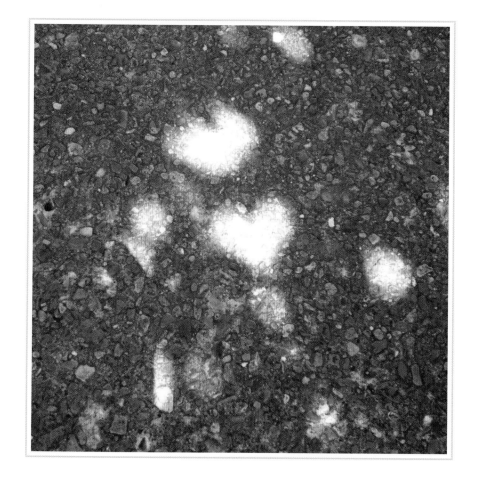

My life-giving love will fuel you
to reach your highest potential.

As you rest in My love and allow Me to fight your battles, your worries will melt away...

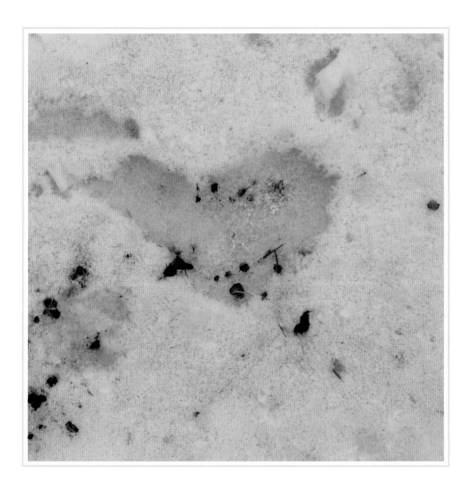

and you will find a
covering of peace.

Even when your heart is
fragile and weary, you will
not be overcome...

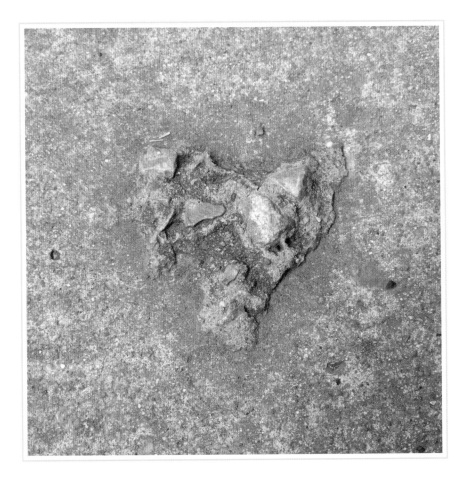

because My love is always
there to ground you…

and you will shine
with the light of My glory
for the world to see.

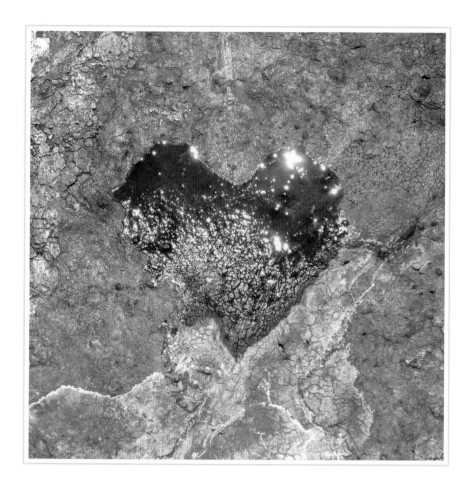

grounded in His *love*

"For I know the plans I have for you,"
declares the Lord, "plans to prosper you and not
to harm you, plans to give you hope and a future.
Then you will call on me and come and pray to me,
and I will listen to you. You will seek me and find
me when you seek me with all your heart."

Jeremiah 29:11-13

about the author

Connie Smith grew up in Nashville, Tennessee. She graduated from the University of Tennessee in 1994 with a degree in Marketing and has spent most of her professional career in Nashville in the healthcare and publishing industries. After resigning as an executive in 2009 to pursue a business venture that did not unfold as she had hoped, she suddenly found herself in a desolate place. In part, this began a quest to connect with God in a deeper way and, ultimately, to find her purpose. Little did she know the journey itself would produce the elements for a project she would later discover to be her sought-after passion. *Never Lose Heart* was born out of this journey in 2014 and marked her debut as an inspirational writer. Two years later, she published *Grounded in His Love*, the follow-up to *Never Lose Heart.* In addition to her love for writing, Connie enjoys spending time with family and friends, leading Bible study discussion groups at her home, cooking and entertaining, art, hiking, nature, and being outdoors.

share your photos

Have you seen a heart? We would love for you to share it with us! Please email your photo to connie@neverloseheart.com, along with your permission to include it in Never Lose Heart's Community Gallery at www.neverloseheart.com.

To receive information about book-signing events, special promotions, and new products/book projects, please sign up for our newsletter at www.neverloseheart.com. To book Connie for your event, please contact her at connie@neverloseheart.com.

Follow us:

@neverloseheartbook

For a study resource on the themes expressed in this book, please go to www.neverloseheart.com to download a list of the scripture references that inspired this book.